For the
BRIGHT ONES

May they come out of the shadows

by
Sarah Ann Negus

© 2022 Sarah Negus

All rights reserved. No portion of this book may be reproduced in any form without permission from the publisher, except as permitted by copyright law.

For permissions contact:
sarah@sarahnegus.com

Cover design by: Natasa Ivancevic
Artwork by: www.jordisarrate.com

Paperback ISBN: 978-1-7370403-6-1
Ebook ISBN: 978-1-7370403-7-8

Published by: Serapis Bey Publishing
Literary Agent and Editor: Wendy Yorke
WRITE. EDIT. PUBLISH
www.wendyyorke.com

Dedication

"Poetry is my longing formed into language
Words collected together on a wave of emotion
Flowing with a tide that reminds me
Of everything I cannot say."

This collection of poems came as a surprise to me.

When something is easy, brings joy and excitement I do more of it and that is what happened here. Poetry has been a life-long pleasure, but usually as a reader. I have dabbled in writing private pieces before, then these came.

Sometimes, there is a meeting of two people that changes everything.

This book is a result of one of those times. The words coming through on the music of a guitar; the notes and melodies acting as a muse; the song as an anchor to hold onto while playing with the creative force that is available to all of us. It opened a channel for me and the words dropped onto the page. Most times, I felt vulnerable to read them, let alone share them, but here they are for you.

My work in the world has always been the work of the heart and of the soul, connecting people to a deeper truth of themselves. Helping people to remember that they are connected to something wonderful and vast. Opening them up to their inner spiritual power. This book is another vehicle for that intention of my life.

May it remind you of your own heart's strength.

Sarah x

Contents List

Energy is everything	1
Innovate they said	2
Where Aphrodite tumbles	3
I wait …	4
Breathe	5
Rapture in the night	6
She holds her gaze upon us	7
How do dreams come true?	8
I confess	9
Are you living life as an adventure or a chore?	10
Stay	11
Do you dare to love a man	13
And maybe it's her presence of self	14
We watch the same moon and the same stars	15
The deepest scar may not be the newest	16
Empty	17
Did you fly too close to the sun	19
Morning glory	20
Into the darkness or is it the light?	21
This man	22
What next?	23
Recovery	24
Ignore me again	25
Don't fall in love with me	26
When I close my eyes	27
I love you already	28

Not quite strangers	29
Planets and stars	30
Life's water flows through your deserts	31
Confident	32
Within me is Tristessa	33
I lay upon the ground	34
Guitar melody	35
Come with me, my darling	36
Who are you, again?	37
A symphony of silence	38
What do I want?	39
Alone	40
When you sit alone	41
67 miles	42
The poet's pen when eloquently guided	43
Never doubt my motives	44
Watching you	45
The island has a rhythm	46
The huntress with her golden arrows sends them flying	47
One day in the warmth of the setting sun	48
I waited	49
Hello	51
Life is a privilege	52
Whoever you are	53
I need you	54
When I say surrender	55
Demon or angel	56

They told me I was crazy	57
We met and I knew	58
Music playing its story in sound	59
I Am Goddess	60
Sometimes	61
The raven weeps	62
Take me somewhere	63
Loneliness is a solitary sadness	64
Ten more days	65
As the world holds steady	66
What is it like to have a daughter?	67
There is a castle	68
There are little drops of love in everything	70
Do your thoughts wander	71
He is the mountain and the valley	72
Time ticks by	73
If time stood still	74
Oh, to be the wind	75
Forget him	76
Once there was a girl	77
Let go	78
Regret is such a strange friend	79
What if	80
Size 9 feet	81
To be available for love	82
I see you and you see me	83
You looked at me	84
If you could take it all back	85

The wisdom of the ages resides within you for your life.	86
I've waited for you	87
I feel empty	88
I have so much to say	89
I cannot tell you how the love seeps through	90
Time	91
The wind screams that change is coming	92
Still standing	93
Are you there?	94
I am waiting	95
Stay with the momentum of onwards	96
Sadness is a constant	97
Watching the sun king rise	98
Real love	99
The dance between us began so effortlessly	100
A summer's day	101
When life is ugly and tears you apart	102
If you love me	103
How do you see me?	104
Let's talk about life.	105
Love is the ocean, the water and rain.	107
How do you love?	108
Awake but still asleep,	109
Romance like roses	110
When everything is lost	111
You touch my mind	112
I am too intense	113

For years I've heard the overwhelming beat of the
invisible Universe 114
The sea roaring 115
Behind my eyes there is nothing but space 116
Energetic mastery awakens the soul 117

Acknowledgements 119
About the Author 121
Contact the Author 123

I love you; but I don't know why...
I love you; no matter what you think.
I love you ... and this love ... breaks me.

Energy is everything
In the space between reality and imagination is being
In the charge between happy and sad is the wave of life
In the mix of desire and motivation is creation
Nothing is as it seems
You have power over everything even if you are unaware
You are the power of everything
Love yourself and you are free.

Innovate they said
As I stared blankly back
Disrupt the force of you
So, I did.

I took all I knew of me
Into the cauldron
And I stirred.

I bubbled and boiled
For this is no easy process
I found anger and joy
Sadness, longing and lust.

And as I unravelled my knots
My blank stare became glossy
And tears fell unequivocally
And slowly out of the black well of me
Emerged something new.

Where Aphrodite* tumbles
And dances with the sun
Diamonds glisten on the waves
Where the turquoise waters run.

Tread softly on the sand
Answer the ocean's call
Poseidon* is waiting
To catch you if you fall.

Dive down beneath the surface
To the secrets that you keep
Give them up to his witness
As the guardian of the deep.

He offers you a chalice
Full of promise
Full of hope
This cup is ever flowing
With the elixir of love.

*Aphrodite, the Greek goddess of love, born 'from the foam'

*Poseidon, the Greek god of the sea

I wait ...
On the waves of love
Watching quietly.

An observer in the mist of time.
My gaze resting softly on your shoulder's curve
And then
Falling oh, so gently down your spine.

Drinking in the shape of you.
Diving into your eyes.
Bathing in your smile.

And, my love unwinds.

I am lost
And I am found
On the waves of love.

Breathe
I AM!
No
Really breathe.
From your intention of life.
Fill yourself with hope.
Open to the moment.
Let. Go.
Be in the space of you.
With simple faith for the next.
And, life comes again.
Breathe.

Rapture in the night
Dancing with the light of love
Rapture of each other.

The breath of another
Touching softly my heart
Yielding, opening, receiving.
Love.

She holds her gaze upon us
And bathes the Earth in reverie
Steady in her constant embrace
Moving oceans
Whispering memories
Her moonshine is the soft tendrils of dreams
Conceived
Unformed
Becoming.

How do dreams come true?
Wondered the child in my mind.

When we live our wishes into being
Said the wise one within.

Can I whisper them to heaven so they are heard more quickly?

No, my love.
For heaven is now.
And heaven is here.
And heaven is you.

I confess
I don't have all my answers
Nor my ducks lined in a row.

I confess
I'm not all that together
Even though you all think so.

I confess
I feel uneasy
With not knowing which way to turn.

With my over-thinking pattern
So difficult to unlearn.

Confessions feel so vulnerable to share.
Yet once the words are spoken
There is a lightness in the air.

Are you living life as an adventure or a chore?
Do you paddle through the open water
Simply looking for the shore?

Or are you waiting for the whale
To come and take you into awe?

Can you slip beneath the surface of the ocean
Dive down into the depths of the love that is you
And bravely stand with devotion
Facing the destiny lodged in your heart?
Revealed moment by moment
And day to day
As you evolve
Inviting you to hold the vision
Innovate your plan.

Wherever you are.
Whoever you be.
Whatever you do.

Your imagination cannot yet design all that is waiting for you.

Stay
Don't leave
Be here
Be present

Stay
With me
In the mirror of my eyes

Stay
And see
The past melting away
Removing its grip
So, you can be free

Stay
It is safe
Within my arms
They will hold you
While you weep

Stay
Find relief
From the effort of living
In this heart that is open
And waiting to give

Stay
Don't leave
Be here
Be present
I am steady
I will heal you
I will open your wings

Stay

Do you dare to love a man
Deep in your bones
Wide in your heart
With your very being?

Do you dare to love a man
Who wears his battle scars
Upon his heart
And carries his broken wings
On his back untended?

Will you love a man again
And hold him while he heals
Knowing this is the only way to wholeness?

Will you offer him this love
That moves the Earth
And ignites the stars
And carries such promise?

Will you turn away from fear
Overcome rejection
As you wait
Certain
That he is the one?

I will, she says
And she does.

And maybe it's her presence of self
And her faith in you
To figure it out
And find what's true

And maybe it's the light in her eyes
And the depths of her darkness
That terrifies yet beckons
And shines through

And then without any doubt
It's the visceral beauty of love
Embodied in a woman
Who's full grown and whole.

That is always the ultimate prize.

We watch the same moon and the same stars
You and I
And feel the same sunshine upon our backs
We live beneath the same clouds
As they bust and burst with rain.

This knowing is peace for me
Like the ever-observing tree
Watching
Waiting
Being
As the world goes around.

Love beneath the skies ...

The deepest scar may not be the newest
The newest evoking the deepest

Rejection
Betrayal
Misunderstanding
When love turns to hate
And what was perfection is gone
The deepest scar rises up
And it hurts.

Empty
I don't have the words
They are stuck
Inadequate
Small
This feeling is beyond my language.

I search my mind
I wait for the voice
Absent
Nothing
Silence
The feeling grows in this void of description.

Spiralling out of my heart
Illuminating my eyes
Bringing a hum to my skin
A quickening of my energy.

There is a rush from within
An urge of becoming
My questions bombard my soul
But the words
Don't come.

For this is only mine
An inner sense of love
And the purpose of life.

The One
The vastness
The No-thing
And the everything.

I Am
So tiny in this mix of chaos
So powerful that the heavens roar my name
And whisper my fate to the spirit of life.

There are no words
For none can describe the mystical love I have.

I search for my people
My person
My One
To see if they, he, knows my heart
For when he holds out his hand
Without any words, but a feeling, a truth and a recognition
I'll know without any doubt
He is my man.

Did you fly too close to the sun
And fall from the atmosphere
In the death throes of ecstasy?
Were you blinded by his flame?
Did you tumble and roll?
With the pain of knowing you could do nothing more
And still wish to fly again
Caught in the memory of
Lies and manipulation
Tricked and deceived by your own imagination
Led along your path
As a lamb walks
Innocent and trusting
Naïve and playful
In love
In promise
In hope
With faith
To be cut down
Suddenly
By your own higher purpose
For this road
Was a gifted lesson
Hard learned
Never copied
Nor repeated
Yet, still you yearn for the sun.

Morning glory
Amid the chorus of dawn
Soft eyed and sleepy
Gently touching
Finding our place to land
In this day

Morning glory
Deep connection
Eyes closed and awakening
Heart to heart
Remembering
You are human

Into the darkness or is it the light?
Into my blindness or is it my sight?
Out of illusion and into the truth
Searching for something without any proof.

Under the surface to what lies beneath
I find my beauty, my spirit, my force.
Hidden and hiding
Timid and shy
To openly speak
Let alone fly
This beauty I've found
Was here all along
Muted
Quiet
Awaiting her time.
Emerging reformed
Wearing new clothes
Beating her drum
No stumble
Or tremble
Simply walking in love.

This man
The only man
Who has looked into my eyes,
Deeply, directly

This man
The only man
Unafraid of my heart
He holds me
Adores me
Sure of his part.

Our lives intertwine
It's always been so
Despite the twists and the turns we lived
So, we could know
Our own souls connect
With the power of love.

This man
The only man
Sent for me to love.

What next?
Be still my darling
Be still

Be the deep pool of water
Captured by the land
Beneath the warm sun
And the cool moon

Be the rushing water
Of the stream
Becoming a river
A sea
An ocean

Be the rain
That covers the land
Be that wet
That he cannot stand

Be the drops of dew
And the soft mist
Be the clouds that are full
Be the life-giving drink

Be fluid my darling
In all of these things
Be silence
Be potent
Be joy
Be bliss

Recovery
Recovering
Isn't this something we do each day
Recovering our lost pieces
So, we can grow and play
Recovery seems never ending
Consistent
Ongoing
From our first breath
Our first step
On our life-long road to recovery.

Ignore me again
I really don't mind
For I know my missives
Are read and bring smiles.

Find other things
More pressing than me
Don't think of me
You idiot
Still lost in your past
This nothing
Is something
And time is moving fast.

I'm patient
I know things
Stop hiding
Behind all you think is so dear
The one thing
Available
To heal you is here.

I'm standing right here
About as big as a bus
Waving and jumping
And shouting
And waiting
For you to say, Yes, to us!

Don't fall in love with me
There is no way back.
It's a honey trap
A beautiful game
A wink in the dark
An erotic dream.

Don't fall in love with me
I mean it
I do!
I'm elegantly quirky,
Cosmic
Divine.

Don't fall in love with me.

When I close my eyes
I see you
Standing in my doorway.

When I listen in the dark
I hear you
Breathing next to me.

When I dream, I feel you
Skin to skin
Reality?
Illusion?
Imagination?
Experience?

When you talk with me
I am here

When you sing to me
Seduced.

When you live your life
I miss you in mine.

I love you already
I loved you before
I love you now
Always
My whole life
The deep in your eyes
The black of your hair
The smile I recognise
Your vulnerability
Your strength
Your creativity that makes me belong
To you
Your voice
Your words
Your energy and truth
I love you
Before I know you

Not quite strangers
Not quite lovers
Friends dressed in false clothes
A tuxedo
A ballgown
Waiting
At the foot of a staircase
Leading to the main event
Do you dare to take my hand
To dance among the starlit ballroom
No longer in disguise?

Planets and stars
Moments and lifetimes
Music and words
Heart and soul

Little things that touch you
And forever change you
Welcome them
Search for them

The unexpected
The refreshing
The kindred spirit
Those you know but have not yet met

Call them to you
Gather them around you
Drown in the waters of life and connection

Life's water flows through your deserts
If you wait and notice the small things
And follow the channel they carve you'll see an oasis
No illusion
It comes from the heat of you
A haven to enjoy
Drink here among the trees and the fauna
Fill yourself up

Love those you meet
For they are soul messengers
Sent by you
To you
To help you remember
To live
To smile
To love even when you think you cannot

Confident
Beautiful
Playful
Curious
Intense

She dances in the magic realms of Maya*
The place between now and then
She plays with the silence
Singing music only you can hear
Forever under a celestial gaze
Of omnipotent wonder
She is She.

*Maya, a sanksrit word referring to 'the veil' creating the illusion that our world is real and separate to the spiritual realms

Within me is Tristessa*

A beauty shrouded in grey
Worn heavy by the clinging memories
Of another day

She lost her heart you see
Once when the sun shone bright
The smiling rose of her lips
Forever more set sharp

Tristessa hides a secret
One she's kept for years and years
She holds it in a wooden box
Buried full of all her fears
Sometimes she hears a knocking
A fist upon the wood
The slow steady beat
Of insistence
That now it is time to live.

Tristessa is a character from a famous novel of the same name written by Jack Kerouac. He created the name from the Spanish and Portuguese word 'tristeza' meaning sadness

I lay upon the ground

A bed damp and strong
I gaze up through the trees
As twilight descends
Watching and waiting for
The nightingale's song
She hears my silent ask
And her voice rings clear and true
The world turns slowly
The moon comes into view
This night I am treated
To a sight that floods my eyes
Not only our closest cousin's face
But Venus' twinkling guise
She is low upon the horizon
Becoming brighter in the sky
The planet of love rises
To kiss the light goodbye
I am in awe
Cradled by the Earth
Covered by the heavens
So small am I, yet
I know my watching impacts us all
For no other ever
Will behold the sights I do
Nor smell the fragrance of the night
As he drops his veil
All the time I hold this wonder
In my heart, my inner eye
The world is changed, uplifted, still turning
And everything is good.

Guitar melody
Languid and cool
A twilight breeze
Rippling a moonlit pool.

A mirror to your soul
Winks once and then winks twice
As the music
Tricks your mind to relax and know that
Inner truth is the prize.

Come with me, my darling
Into the deep dark blue
Hold my hand
And let's discover
All the lies you think are true.

Come with me, my darling
Trust me if you dare
Open your heart
Relax your mind
Strip all your layers bare.

Come with me, my darling
Throw off what you feel is real
There is a rhapsody within you
It is the language of your soul.

Who are you, again?
You say you are my friend
I know you keep me distant
But really, this has got to end.

Friendship has been good
But all I want is more
To be loved
To kiss and laugh with you
And roll around the floor.

Who are you, again?
Oh yes, a friend
It's nothing else and nothing much
Sedate, apart ... nonsense.

I don't believe it's all there is ...
This nothing can evolve
Because nothing is always something.

A symphony of silence
Elegantly true
A waterfall of life
Cascading over you

A footstep in the sand
That often time records
Something new
Something bold
That marks the moment
The shift occurred

What do I want?
To burn in the flame of your eyes
To look away
Shyly
From your gaze
To breathe
To taste love
To touch love
To be filled with the sacred and the holy.

Alone
Not lonely
Space
No box
Anything is possible
Exciting don't you think
Oh, I don't mean you will fly
But maybe you might
A bumble bee can but ...
No one told her otherwise

When you sit alone
Not lonely though, be sure
And start to wonder
Of all the things
Life, cancer and the cure.

Or how to feed the starving
Or bring fresh water through the dust
Or even how
The people here
Can smile and laugh and live together as one.

Remember ...
There are no edges to the ideas you bring through
Only how, and when, and who can I be and what can I do.

67 miles
The space from here to there
Quite a distance
I am told
Although I'm not sure that is fair

Or is it a reason
Not to connect
To stay safe
To stay free
In the pain of loneliness

A change means
Facing dragons
The ones that guard your heart
Such dragons fly in one wing beat
The 67 miles that we're apart

I see them all around you
Firing up your need to succeed
But such efforts
Will undo you
Because your heart is left to bleed

The poet's pen when eloquently guided
Is a force, like no other.
It opens up the fissures
In the thickest walls of ice built around any heart.
Her ink still wet upon the page
A medium who touches where nothing else can.
Not a drip or a rivulet
But a torrent that washes away all your desire
Until ...
At the end of the verse
You are left
Bare
Emotionally connected
Raw
Yet beautiful
Knowing you were seen.
And then that penmanship
Thrusts through your amour
And pierces your heart.

Never doubt my motives
Ignore them perhaps, if you can.
But love when offered unconditionally
Is the measure of a woman.
It fills the silent void
Bridges the gap between worlds
Heals old wounds
And follows new maps.
Brings the undiscovered into knowing
And the hidden into sight.
When love is offered blindly
Without its landing in plain sight
It is a power you cannot hold
Surrender
Without a fight.

Watching you
The bright one, is a practice in patience
Knowing your fame in my heart has me completely undone
Waiting with you to catch our star
Something that only happens once
Wanting this connection
Completely
Through to my very soul

The island* has a rhythm
A beat within its land.
Listen well and you'll hear it
Reach out to take its hand.

Never underestimate its power or its voice.
Many have and burned their truth
And lost their will and choice.

For sirens hold its energy
Their song a deadly scream.
Unless you know your own one
You'll get lost within their dream.

*Ibiza my spiritual home

The huntress with her golden arrows sends them flying
Through the sky
Ablaze with sunlight aiming true, aiming high.

Artemis* stands so firmly feet planted on the Earth
Her armour falling now
Her body gloriously bare.

She demands you choose to send your heart's wishes
As potent intentions
Into the Universe.

Give them up, she whispers.
Her voice the breeze through the trees.
Let me carry all your dreams in the chariot with me.

Artemis goddess of the hunt in Greek Mythology, named Diana by the Romans

One day in the warmth of the setting sun
She decided no more hiding from love.
She waited as the sky glowed pink, magenta, grey
And let the colours soothe her frightened heart.

And, suddenly, in the last moments of the day
The light flashed green and she opened to her dream
Held in the coming moonshine.

The dream, to be safe, walking upon the Earth
Left foot leading
Answering the call, to be touched, of heart, of body, of mind.

And as the half-light enveloped her
And she waited for the heady black of night
She finally
Surrendered.

I waited
On the corner
By the green door
Under the street lamp
Looking towards the edge of town
Moments turn to minutes and then hours and weeks
Then days and months.

You never came
And
All the hope dropped down from my heart to my toes
And sank into the cold Earth beneath my feet.

Still, I waited
In disbelief.

You didn't see me?
Or perhaps you did
Yet couldn't hold my gaze for long
Instead, running to hide from the promise of something good
Of beauty
Of truth
Of both?

Just in case
I waited some more
A little longer, I thought.
That is all he needs
Time will show the way

And so, I waited believing in myself
And then wondering
Could I have got it
All upside down?

And I searched out again, looking towards
the edge of town
Where the wind whistled
And the light faded
And you never came.

Hello
Hey
Hi
Remember me
The woman who drank pink gin with a silver rim
And chenin blanc and laughed a while with you.

Hello
Hey
Hi
It's me
Again
Wanting to start anew
What began when
You smiled hello
And I remembered that butterflies do exist.

Life is a privilege
Life is a beauty
Life is a joy
It holds secrets.

As you breathe, into each moment of yourself,
Life is a roaring storm carrying a cacophony of music.
As it rains
Life is the exquisite dance of sunlight upon your back

And ...

Life's intention is held in your heart.
Only when you dare to open it
Is life truly lived.

Whoever you are
There will always be the One
Who stops you in your tracks.
A course correction
A storm
A flood
The one who opens your heart
And quickens your blood.
Who makes you love,
With a passion you have never known
Only to leave ...
Betray ...
Reject ...
And totally break you.
The one who shows you how lost you are
The one who, by leaving
Allows you to be found.

I need you
That deeply vulnerable declaration,
Which means I trust you
To catch me when I fall
And to lift me higher than I can go alone,
To see the truth of me
Always.
I need you
That deeply vulnerable declaration
Which requires your love.

When I say surrender
Do not sink into the abyss
Surrender is a skill.
Something that many cannot do.
It takes the heart of a lion
And the inner dove of faith.
Surrender
And let go
Of all you know you are
Lay back
Open
To the light that is coming through.
Surrender means you have tried it all
And you can see without a view.
Surrender to the grander plan
And watch the light come through.

Demon or angel
Which one are you?
I am in so deep.
Do your worst
And your best.
Let me love you.

They told me I was crazy
I knew I was in love.
They watched and judged my patience
And I held steady in my heart.
They shook their heads and rolled their eyes.
But I knew my inner truth,
Some people are worth the wait ...
And that is you, my love.

We met and I knew
My pathway had opened
All the ones before made such sense
The lovers who held my hand
While I learned all I needed
To be able to love me
So I can now, love you.

Music playing its story in sound
A picture emerges
And entwines all around
Evocative
Hypnotic
It takes me to trance
I hold back
Afraid
Can I let myself dance?
The music continues
Its story untold
Wanting me to write
The words that it holds

I Am Goddess
Love me.

Fall into the space in my soul
I am all you will ever need
Embodied here and now.
Come with me and you will
Know the riches of all you are
Dive into me and you will find your true nature.

I Am Goddess
Love me.

Sometimes
The woman stands confident and brave
But deep within her inner world
The little girl is afraid.

She shies away from conflict
Plays havoc with her truth.

She wants to ride the swing that flies
The one that feels so free
But hesitates
Looks back
Waits.

Not sure who she will be
For flying high
Takes courage.
It takes a steady grip
And more than that
In every way
It takes an inner knowing of
The little girl, that's me.

The raven weeps
The dove awaits
The eagle soars above.
Each feathered friend
Who comes to me,
A messenger of hope.

Take me somewhere
Without knowing where
Somewhere without Earthly boundaries
Let's touch the magic of the stars together
And get lost in our own sense of freedom

Loneliness is a solitary sadness
It isolates you from love
Separates you from the future
Divides you into pieces
And waits
While you circumnavigate the globe of your heart
Creating a picture with the jigsaw of your past
A masterpiece
Worth the living

Ten more days
That's 240 hours
Less now,
Time passes while I write
And time is precious
And so is love.

Ten more days
Until
Who knows?
A beginning,
An ending,
Or both?

Ten more days
That's 240 hours
Less now,
Time passes while I think.
These words have meaning
At least to me
And chart my feelings,
Hopes and dreams
Ten more days
To wait.

As the world holds steady
On the day it turns around
Its energy deeply darkens
All our landscapes all our towns
And in this quiet holding
With winter wrapped tightly through
The birth of something new occurs
In our hearts and then, our minds
Hope flutters
Dreams unfold
A New Year beckons
Close the windows to the past
Sweep out the dusts of regret
For though the Earth has stopped this night
Its turning cannot end
And life will push
And life will yearn
To grow ... up and out and forward
So, as the world holds steady
This solstice is our chance
To dive within our own deep darkness
And turn our lives around

What is it like to have a daughter?
As a father
As a man?
The most beautiful of children,
Held tightly in your hands.
You watch her cry,
You watch her smile,
All innocent and true.
And as she grows to womanhood
She teaches you
About you.

There is a castle
Within a fortress
Dark and forbidding
Hidden in the mist.

There is a well
And a window
And a silent song.

Listen with your inner ear
Its music will lead you on
Down a twisted staircase
Through the seven levels
Of your mind
To the secret place
The part of you
Buried deeply
Under the layers of your life.

It rumbles and is restless
It finds its voice and roars.

She moves the Earth
And all that you have built, falls.
The castle
The fortress
Are no more.

The twisted staircase exposed
And then,
Without fanfare
The truth of you arises
The light rips through the gloam
And out of the darkest of nights
You emerge ... reborn.

There are little drops of love in everything
In a smile
In a tear
In a belly laugh
And a sob.
Sometimes we are overcome with fear
Or anger or regret
But trust me
There are
Little drops of love in everything.

Do your thoughts wander
To the edge of all that is known?
Do they try each closed door
And find one that is ajar?
Do you have an ethereal gaze
That promises magic
Amongst their beautiful haze?
Do you adventure where no others tread
To the farthest reaches of the Universe
While lying still
Safe in your bed?

He is the mountain and the valley
The snow-capped summit
And the devil's run.
My challenge and all my fears.
He has kept me waiting all these years.

He is the ocean and the shore
The gentle waves
And the tidal roar.
He is the shallow and the deep.
So close, yet out of reach.

He is the forest and the plane
The Lebanon cedar
The lion's mane.
He is everything I've ever known.
The greatest voyage.
My absolute home.

Time ticks by
You cannot hear it, but it is constant
Blink an eye
And its thief has snatched another moment.

It rushes past
And life trickles through
Its cracks and crannies
Leaving only memories
Of all you have had to do.

Time is your friend
Your enemy
A beast
For time is your ever-loving companion
Never leaving time to breathe.

If time stood still
And looked at this beautiful place where we are
I wonder ...
Would it make such haste,
With all these amazing things?

Or would it stop ...
And be in love
And unwind from its constant motion
So, it could feel
My precious heart,
Beating.

Oh, to be the wind
To have such speed and vision
To clear the past so suddenly
No regret
No apology.

Oh, to be the rain
And wash away the pain
To rise above what has been felt
And leave a heart so bare.

Oh, to be the sun
And bring hope to us once more
Its warmth and its fire
To light us up, anew.

Forget him
The one who doesn't want you.

Forgive him
The one who cannot see you.

Forsake him
And unlock your heart from his.

Open the door
Look ahead for something new.

Feel the door closing softly
No glances back.

Leave him there
Forgotten, forgiven, forsaken.

Once there was a girl
She lived in a colourful land of hopes and dreams
And faeries and stars and she had a promise to keep

Once there was a way
To live and still be free to journey to the beauty
Of the place beyond the veil

Then once
And that is all it took
Life turned dark, the light hidden and small
Until the girl all grown, cracked open and fell
Back to Earth, back to beyond the veil and
back into herself.

Let go
And
Then
Let in
Something better
Something more for you
Much more true

Let go
And
Smile
With love
For all that was

Let go
And
Reach
Beyond
Your own limits

For it is in the stretch of ourselves
That we are found

Regret is such a strange friend
It requires a backward glance
And an observer's view
Of what ...
Of who ...
Of when ...
You could, or should have been, something other than you.

Regret holds heavy
Around your heart
And lets sadness filter through on every thought
Affirming that
You could, or should have done, something
other than you.

What if
I am you
And everything I see is me?

Then all you bring
I already have
And I've summoned you to make that real.

Size 9 feet
Trample heavy footed
Across the landscape of my heart

Right foot landing
Without any single moment
Of awareness

Lost in a perfect storm
No compassion to stop the tread of your shoes
Imprinting their shape on my soul

To be available for love
You must first trust
That love is kind
And love will heal
And love is all around

I see you and you see me
Our interest and excitement are between us
Our energy rises together
And life is glistening with presence.

We ebb and flow
In love with each other
And challenge our hearts to grow.

We share
We dance
We hold and soothe
Our love is like no other.

You looked at me
Your eyes ablaze
I looked away, afraid.

But in that moment
You shook my dreams awake.

If you could take it all back
Undo the stitches of time
Change everything, would you?

I shrugged
I didn't know then, though I might
have whispered, Yes.

But now
As life has layered upon me
I know I'd live it all again
For I am lighter
Because of its darkness
And my life brighter
Because of its terrible fire.

The wisdom of the ages resides within you for your life.
All you need to find is the time and the inclination
To dive into the depths of your inner world.

All you need is to offer yourself the same investment
As you would the assets in your business.

All you need is to cut yourself some slack
And put yourself first.

You are the one who makes your life happen,
after all.

I've waited for you
All my days have passed by
I have been mistaken
Before
By a few
But now
I both drown and am burned
By the look in your eyes
And my soul stops
And sighs
It is you.

I feel empty
Disbelieving
Incredibly sad
Lonely
Nothing seems worth doing
Because everything worth having
Is slightly out of reach
Not available to me.

I feel stuck
Waiting
In a holding pattern
Even if I venture out, am busy
The feeling remains

I feel regret
Stupid
Why did I meet him?

I am worthy of more
There is something better
Just there …
Around the corner
Out of sight
Connected to your heart.

I have so much to say
Say it

I have so much to ask
Ask it

But it falls on deaf ears
And walls of ice
These are your own.

Listen
Melt the ice around your heart
It aches so,
Because its glacier of safety
Is too heavy to carry.
Melt the past away
Watch it leave you.

Instead ...
Drop
By little drop ...
Allow love to warm you.

I cannot tell you how the love seeps through
But it does
With the sunshine and the moonshine
Through the starlight
And the planets' gaze

I cannot tell you how the love seeps through
But it does
Through a voice
And a song
Or a melody
Touching your heart
Speaking with your soul

I cannot tell you how the love seeps through
But it does
With a smile
Or a touch
A kind word,
And a twinkling eye

I cannot tell you how the love seeps through
But it does
Because love is the way of life
It turns the world
Builds the Universe

I cannot tell you how the love seeps through
But it does.

Time
Hope
Faith
Living all you can.

Connection
Chemistry
Excitement
Living all you will.

Patience
Surrender
Trust
Making sense of the path.

The wind screams that change is coming
Hide, find shelter, think you will ride it out?
But
There is no escaping
The wind of change
Its turbulent power rages over the landscape
Ripping up the stuck, the old, the dead.
No guide, nor angel's hand will reach you
To soften its fierce song
For the roaring wind
Comes when all your dances are done.

Still standing
Despite your cruel sword.

Still walking
My steps a little faltered.

Still exploring
All that lies ahead.

Still breathing in the love of our world.

Are you there?
In the night
Beside me.

Are you there?
In the day
Holding me tight.

Are you there?
When I cry
To catch my tears.

Are you there?
When I feel
I cannot survive.

Are you there?
When I am behaving badly
And steady me
Without judgement.

Are you there?
When I laugh
To join in my joy.

Are you there?
Are you there?
Are you there?

I am waiting
Holding my breath with anticipation
For the day when you say
I am come.

Stay with the momentum of onwards
Surrender
Be intentional with where you want to go.

Let the past be past
Remove its present power
Nothing there will ever change
Not a single minute or hour.

Life's gifts, my darling
Are always hard to bear
A breath ...
A heartbeat ...
And actions so unfair

Sadness is a constant
For what is lost
And what is dead
But sadness has its own beauty
For without it you would not have lived.

Grief and loneliness
Companions to the end
For when a loved life leaves
There is nothing left to comprehend.

Only moving through the process
Knowing this too will pass
And once again
You'll be ready
For what is just along your path.

Watching the sun king rise
Waiting for its warming touch
As it stretches across the sky
A new day awakes
And life moves on
What will you make,
Of our sun's new song?

Real love
That state we search for

Real love
Never knowing how it feels

Real love
A moment
A heartbeat
A frequency that never leaves

Maybe sometimes somewhat
Numbed
Never quite gone

The dance between us began so effortlessly
One step
A twirl
A smile
The music played and we laughed
While we perfected our style

Our frame evolved
You led
I followed
We fell
We paused
And then began again
The dance between us stronger now
More beautiful

A summer's day
The air laden with ripeness
The sky an atmosphere of blue
With clouds of angel's breath dancing in the altitude
Magnificence
In the abundance of life

When life is ugly and tears you apart
Love it more
When the world cracks you open and everything falls away
Love it hard
When the sky breaks all around you and the stars are hidden from view
Love it most

For love changes all things
From the inside out
And love is the light held in your heart
Love always

If you love me
You will know the strength I have

If you love me
You will see the fear I hide

If you love me
You will find the touch of my soul

If you love me
You will find all you thought was lost

How do you see me?
Through fractured and dimmed eyes.
How do I see you?
As a precious light.

How do you feel me?
Behind a barrier of fear.
How do I feel you?
With all my senses.

How do you know me?
With all of your judgement.
How do I know you?
As a spiritual spark.

How do you love me?
Like a bird in a cage.
How do I love you?
With the wings of my heart.

Let's talk about life.
How precious it is.
It is always this now
And it is with such a small viewpoint
that we stagger and blunder, tumble along
Holding our breath, awaiting our death.

Vulnerable
Arrogant
Afeared
Confident
Blazé
Complacent

Let's talk about life.
How precious it is.
It is always this now
And if we look up and look forward
Our breath becomes measured
And steady and strong.

Surviving
Processing
Feeling
Loving
Thriving
Living
Experiencing
Evolving in truth.

Let's talk about life.
How precious it is.
It is always this now
And it is grander than you.

It is
The animals
The insects
The fish and the trees
The fauna
The air
The Earth
The sky and the breeze

Let's talk about life.
How precious it is.
It is always this now
We are custodians of its peace.

Honoured
Promised
Accepted
Recognised
Acknowledged
Embodied

Let's talk about life.
How precious it is.
It is always this now
How much can you BE?

Love is the ocean, the water and rain.
It is life giving light and death bringing dark.
Love is the answer, over said but so true.
Love is the basis of me and of you.

Love is creation, motivation and genius
It is the perfect quality,
Abject distortion
And all in-between.

Love is the monster, the beauty, the sinner and saint.
The beast and the maiden, the crone and the mage.
Love is the frequency of quickening within.
It is the leader, the loser and all those who win.

Love is the courage, the journey, the path.
Love is the question you are too afraid to ask.
Love is your baby, the infant, your child.
Love is the adult, the innocent and the wise.

Love is ...

How do you love?
With your heart or your mind?
Is love a concept you are hoping to find?

Love is your being
It is a state within
And love is the way we create what we live.

Lean into your truth here
Be brave with your words
How can you love those who live in this world?

Not only the people we hold so dear
But all living beings, our planet, all in our sphere.

Love is creation, evolution, motivation
And love is the energy behind every action.

Love
Love
Love

Awake but still asleep,
My dream pulls at my mind.
A door appears inviting me to find my way
This space so far unknown,
A place of growth and of change.

Where there is a crone,
A wise woman bent over, grey-haired and kind.
She looks at me nodding,
She's been waiting for a while.

I heard her whisper years ago.
"Sarah," she said, "it is time."
I shook her words away from me,
I ran, closed down, denied.

But as the time ticks on,
Its straight line pointing true.
There came this day
When I wanted more
Of me, of us, of you.

She holds my life and all I've learned
And mixes it you see
With everything there has ever been
In you, in us, in me.

The child within has found her home
The girl has settled down.
The mother is someone I know well
And I wear the goddess gown.

And now I wait, awake yet still asleep
For the crone to pass her crown.

Romance like roses
Chocolates and wine
Give them to another
Make your heart mine

Safe hands
Warm arms
Open heart
Soul connection

This is romance.

When everything is lost
And everyone has gone
The only thing left is you
Here you'll find the battle with your mind
Until the time when that is lost too
For when you give up
And that day will come
All that remains is your soul
That day, is a good day
From there everything will be found
And everyone will arrive

You touch my mind
And I fall
Deep into the darkness of my soul.

You touch my heart
And I rise
High into the light of my life.

I am too intense
It scares them
Sometimes me too
But when all I feel
Is so alive and strong
To dumb it down
Would be wrong

For years I've heard the overwhelming beat of the invisible Universe

It covers me when I am still
A blanket of nothingness
That sinks through my skin and deafens my ears
And enraptures my mind

For years I've been afraid wanting it gone
Muffling its song
Numbing my skin to its hum

But now, as I'm older and longer lived
I've taken to waiting and wanting
And wanting and waiting for the silence to land

And when she does
She holds me so gently and I know I'm free

This intelligent force
This light of intent
Slowly wraps around all I Am

She calms my soul
She brings me peace
She is my power
And absolute grace

The sea roaring
The wind racing
Cloud cathedrals billowing
A scene of nature's chaos opening the space
Between sky and horizon
Where the light comes through
And love arrives ...

Behind my eyes there is nothing but space
Where all of reality seems so far away
The constant noise of living
Silenced

Behind my eyes there is everything in space
Where all illusions fade
And my voice of truth exists

Behind my eyes I find both hope and peace
A coming home to myself
Coupled with an urge to exist

Behind my eyes my sense of myself grows
Until I know I must return
And live

Energetic mastery awakens the soul
Exploring depths of lived experience

Exploding myths of immature perspective

Bringing freedom of choice to every moment of living

And the vibration of love into creation.

Acknowledgements

Gratitude to all the poets greater than me who have left their love in the world for all to see.

"Perhaps all the dragons in our lives are princesses who are only waiting to see us act, just once, with beauty and courage. Perhaps everything that frightens us is, in its deepest essence, something helpless that wants our love."

Rainer Maria Rilke, *Letters to a young poet*

This book of mine would never have found its way onto the page without Wendy Yorke, my editor and literary agent. She found the thread running through my jumble of words and helped me land these pieces of my heart on the page. My gratitude is immense. Thank you!

About the Author

Sarah Ann Negus is a modern day shaman, spiritual mentor and executive coach, writer and public speaker. She grew up in south London and has spent her life finding out who she really is. As a child Sarah learned that not everyone saw what she did and she hid her gifts. Coming back to them as an adult, she slowly remembered her purpose and promised to share them.

Sarah runs a successful mentoring and public speaking business, working with entrepreneurs and executives who understand that their energy is a powerful driving force for growth, both personally and professionally. She facilitates an altered state of consciousness for her clients, who observe themselves and the world differently as a result, taking actions from a new belief system, which empowers them to achieve what they previously believed was impossible. Her clients typically say; "Working with Sarah has been life-changing".

Contact the Author

If these poems have touched you, you can find out more about Sarah as below.

Facebook online community
https://www.facebook.com/sarahannnegus/

YouTube Channel
https://www.youtube.com/channel/UCZOtKyGOJzTbUrdJoOO1oLw

LinkedIn
https://www.linkedin.com/in/sarah-negus-0683857/

Pinterest
https://www.pinterest.co.uk/sarahnegus/pins/

Instagram

https://www.instagram.com/sarahannnegus/?hl=en

@ModernDayShaman®
All links to these resources can also be found on Sarah's website
www.sarahnegus.com

www.ingramcontent.com/pod-product-compliance
Lightning Source LLC
Chambersburg PA
CBHW050208130526
44590CB00043B/3220